The Word Wizard's Book of VERBS

Robin Johnson

Crabtree
Publishing
Company
www.crabtreebooks.com

Word Wizard

Author
Robin Johnson

Publishing plan research and development
Reagan Miller, Crabtree Publishing Company

Editorial director
Kathy Middleton

Project coordinator
Kelly Spence

Editor
Anastasia Suen

Proofreader and indexer
Wendy Scavuzzo

Photo research
Robin Johnson, Katherine Berti

Design & prepress
Katherine Berti

Print coordinator
Katherine Berti

Photographs
All images from Shutterstock

Library and Archives Canada Cataloguing in Publication

Johnson, Robin (Robin R.), author
    The word wizard's book of verbs / Robin Johnson.

(Word wizard)
Issued in print and electronic formats.
ISBN 978-0-7787-1292-3 (bound).--ISBN 978-0-7787-1310-4 (pbk.).--
ISBN 978-1-4271-7761-2 (pdf).--ISBN 978-1-4271-7757-5 (html)

    1. English language--Verb--Juvenile literature. I. Title.

PE1271.J54 2014   j428.2   C2014-903819-4
                                          C2014-903820-8

Library of Congress Cataloging-in-Publication Data

Johnson, Robin (Robin R.) author.
  The Word Wizard's book of verbs / Robin Johnson.
     p. cm. -- (Word Wizard)
  Includes index.
  ISBN 978-0-7787-1292-3 (reinforced library binding) --
ISBN 978-0-7787-1310-4 (pbk.) -- ISBN 978-1-4271-7761-2 (electronic pdf) --
ISBN 978-1-4271-7757-5 (electronic html)
  1. English language--Verb--Juvenile literature. 2. English language--Parts of speech--Juvenile literature. 3. English language--Grammar--Juvenile literature. I. Title. II. Title: Book of verbs.

  PE1271.J58 2014
  425'.6--dc23
                            2014027800

Crabtree Publishing Company

www.crabtreebooks.com   1-800-387-7650

Printed in the U.S.A./092014/JA20140811

Published in Canada
Crabtree Publishing
616 Welland Ave.
St. Catharines, Ontario
L2M 5V6

Published in the United States
Crabtree Publishing
PMB 59051
350 Fifth Avenue, 59th Floor
New York, New York 10118

Published in the United Kingdom
Crabtree Publishing
Maritime House
Basin Road North, Hove
BN41 1WR

Published in Australia
Crabtree Publishing
3 Charles Street
Coburg North
VIC 3058

Contents

Magic words

Words work magic! They send you over rainbows. They let you wish on stars. Words take you to faraway lands. They bring you home again. You can do anything with words! The Word Wizard wants to make magic with words. Will you help him learn about words called **verbs**?

Useful words

Words work their magic in different ways. Verbs tell us about actions. Words help us go places. They let us share our ideas. Words let us ask questions. They help us find answers. Think of all the ways we use words!

Where will words take you?

What are verbs?

Verbs are action words. They tell us what people or things are doing. The Word Wizard waves her wand. Her bunny disappears! The word "waves" is a verb. It tells us what the wizard is doing. The word "disappears" is also a verb. It tells us what happens to the bunny.

To see or not to see

Some verbs describe actions we can see. You can see a wizard do magic tricks. Other verbs describe actions we cannot see. The Word Wizard likes to learn about verbs. The words "likes" and "learn" are verbs. You cannot see them. They still describe the wizard's actions.

This girl is just like the Word Wizard. She is making her lollipop disappear!

Word Wizard in training

The Word Wizard is pulling words out of a hat. Which oval has verbs? Help the Word Wizard find it!

swim
kick   bounce
read   look   fall
float   squirt

fast
candy   rabbit
table   pretty   up
hat   leg

Verbs in sentences

We join words together to form **sentences**. A sentence is a complete thought or idea. Every sentence needs a verb. Without a verb, there is no action. Is "the dog" a sentence? No, it is not! There is no action. Let us try it again with a verb. "The dog licks my face." That is a sentence.

Subjects and verbs

Every sentence also needs a **subject**. A subject is the person, animal, place, thing, or idea the sentence is about. The word "dog" is a subject. A verb tells us what the subject is doing. The dog barks. The dog wags its tail. The words "barks" and "wags" are verbs.

What is the dog doing? What is the girl doing? Use verbs to describe their actions.

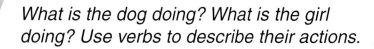

Word Wizard in training

Look at these two captions. Which one is a complete sentence? How do you know? Teach the Word Wizard!

the dog and the boy

The dog is walking the boy!

Verbs must agree

Verbs must agree with subjects in sentences. Some subjects are **singular**. Singular means there is only one. The word "girl" is a singular subject. Singular subjects take singular verbs. Most singular verbs end in "s" or "es." We say, "The girl walks to school. She goes with her friends."

Plural subjects

Other subjects are **plural**. Plural means more than one. The word "girls" is a plural subject. Plural subjects take plural verbs. Most plural verbs do not end in "s." We say, "The girls walk to school. They skip and chat along the way."

Word Wizard in training

Which sentence has the correct verb? Is it singular or plural? The Word Wizard wants to know!

The kids jumps for joy.

The kids jump for joy.

Verb tenses

Verbs can tell us when actions take place. We look at the verb **tense** to find out. The tense of a verb shows the time. Some actions take place right now. We use the **present tense** to show those actions. We say, "The Word Wizard learns about verbs." The word "learns" is in the present tense.

The bear family is climbing a tree.

Past and future

Some actions have already taken place. We use the **past tense** for those actions. Many verbs in the past tense end in "ed." We say, "The Word Wizard learned about verbs last week." Other actions have not taken place yet. We use the **future tense** for those actions. Many verbs in the future tense use "will." We say, "The Word Wizard will learn more about verbs next week."

These kids are going to hide. Will their friend find them?

Irregular verbs

Some verbs do not follow the rules. They are **irregular verbs**. Irregular means they are not like the other verbs. We do not add "ed" to them in the past tense. We form new words instead. You would not say you teached the Word Wizard about verbs. "Teached" is not a word. You would say you taught her instead. "Taught" is the past tense of "teach."

This boy is checking his height. He grew again!

This girl ran and hid behind a tree. Will she be found?

The boy blew some bubbles.

No magic tricks

There is no magic way to learn irregular verbs! You just need to study and remember them. Look at the chart below. It shows some irregular verbs. Do you *think* you can remember them? The Word Wizard *thought* you could!

Present tense	Past tense
is	was
go	went
hide	hid
sit	sat
tell	told
give	gave
take	took
eat	ate
run	ran
grow	grew

Antonyms

Some verbs are **antonyms**. Antonyms are words with totally different meanings. They are also called **opposites**. The verbs "stop" and "go" are antonyms. The verbs "open" and "close" are antonyms. Can you *give* some more antonyms? *Take* your time!

How the world moves

Antonyms help us tell how the world moves. They show us that actions are very different. We stop at red lights. We go at green lights. We open cookie jars. We close them to keep the cookies fresh.

These kids are pulling on a rope. What is an antonym for pulling?

Word Wizard in training

The Word Wizard wants to *learn* some antonyms. Will you *teach* her? Use your finger to match up the opposites.

sit	throw
enter	cry
laugh	find
sink	exit
catch	stand
lose	float

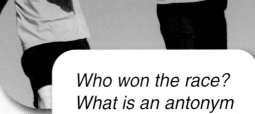

Who won the race? What is an antonym for winning?

Synonyms

Some verbs are **synonyms**. Synonyms mean the same thing or nearly the same thing as other words. The verbs "hop," "jump," and "leap" are synonyms. They are all words with the same meanings.

Not the same old story

Synonyms make stories more interesting. Would you like to hear a story with the same verbs? Would you listen to such a boring book? No, you would not! You would shut the book. You would close it up. Then you would look for another story. You would search for a better book.

These kids are spinning in a park. What is a synonym for spinning?

Word Wizard in training

There are many verbs that tell how you move from place to place. You can walk. You can march. You can stroll. You can prance. How are these verbs different? Act out each way of walking. Strut your stuff and show the Word Wizard your moves!

How are these kids moving? Use synonyms to describe their actions.

Shades of meaning

Some verbs mean almost the same thing. The words "nibble" and "gobble" describe eating. They are not exactly the same, though. "Nibble" means taking little bites. "Gobble" means taking big, fast bites. There are small differences in their meanings. The differences are called **shades of meaning**.

Are these kids jogging, running, or dashing? Will their kite flutter, fly, or soar?

The boy is telling a secret. Is he whispering, talking, or shouting?

Sorting words

Some verbs have weaker meanings. The word "nibble" is a weaker verb. Other verbs have stronger meanings. The word "gobble" is a stronger verb. We can sort words to see their shades of meaning. Then we can choose verbs that tell our stories best.

Weaker words	Stronger words	Strongest words
toss	throw	hurl
nibble	eat	gobble
sip	gulp	guzzle
peek	look	stare
whisper	talk	shout
rinse	clean	scrub
rest	nap	sleep
jog	run	dash

Stay strong

You can pick and choose which verbs to use. Stronger verbs make your stories exciting. You could say the Word Wizard moves her wand. Or you could say she waves her wand. You could say the Word Wizard flies. Or you could say she zooms through the air. Verbs can change your stories like magic!

Word Wizard in training

Now it is your turn to get moving!
Grab some chalk and skip outside.
Draw a comic on the sidewalk.
Make sure it shows some actions.
Write down the actions in your picture.
Use strong verbs to make it exciting.
Then get active and act out the verbs!

What is the chalk family doing? Use verbs to describe their actions.

Learning more

Books

A Backpack Full of Verbs (Words I Know) by Bette Blaisdell. A+ Books, 2014.

Action Words: Verbs (Getting to Grips with Grammar) by Anita Ganeri. Heinemann First Library, 2012.

Home Run Verbs (Grammar All-Stars) by Doris Fisher. Gareth Stevens Publishing, 2008.

Slide and Slurp, Scratch and Burp: More about Verbs (Words Are CATegorical) by Brian P. Cleary. Millbrook Press, 2009.

Verbs (Grammar Basics) by Kate Riggs. Creative Paperbacks, 2013.

Websites

This website has verb lessons, games, quizzes, and pages to print.
www.anglomaniacy.pl/grammar-verbs.htm

Visit this website to spot and pop verbs in a balloon game.
www.softschools.com/language_arts/grammar/verb/balloon_game/

Find the verbs and whack the robots in this fun space game.
www.sheppardsoftware.com/grammar/verbs.htm

Words to know

antonym (AN-tuh-nim) A word that means the opposite of another word

future tense (FYOO-cher tens) The verb form used to describe actions that have not taken place yet

irregular verb (ih-REG-yuh-ler vurb) A verb that changes form in the past tense

opposite (OP-uh-sit) Totally different

past tense (past tens) The verb form used to describe actions that have already taken place

plural (PLOOR-uhl) More than one

present tense (PREZ-uhnt tens) The verb form used to describe actions taking place right now

sentence (SEN-tns) A complete thought or idea

shades of meaning (sheyds uhv MEE-ning) Small differences in the meaning of words

singular (SING-gyuh-ler) Only one

subject (SUHB-jikt) The person, animal, place, thing, or idea a sentence is about

synonym (SIN-uh-nim) A word that means the same thing or nearly the same thing as another word

tense (tens) The form of a verb that shows time

verb (vurb) An action word that tells what people or things are doing

Index